I Am Enough

I Am Enough

Rachael Ann Riley

EVOKE180 PUBLISHING | LAUDERHILL, FL

Rachael Riley/Evoke180 Publishing
Lauderhill, FL
www.evoke180.com

Publisher's Note: This is a work of fiction. Names, characters, places, and incidents are a product of the author's imagination. Locales and public names are sometimes used for atmospheric purposes. Any resemblance to actual people, living or dead, or to businesses, companies, events, institutions, or locales is completely coincidental.

I Am Enough/ Rachael Riley.
ISBN 978-1-7377826-2-9

Scripture quote taken from New American Standard Bible®, Copyright © 1960, 1971, 1977, 1995, 2020 by The Lockman Foundation. All rights reserved.

Printed in USA by 48HrBooks (www.48HrBooks.com)

Dedication

For my mother, Helen;
sister, Jennis; and children, Mario and Imani.

Acknowledgments

My source and Higher Power
My ancestors
My family
My true friends
My publisher, Evoke180 Publishing (Berwick Augustin)

Table of Contents

Foreword

Her presence was remarkable in my eleventh- and twelfth-grade Trinidad classrooms. I well remember—as a young high school teacher more than three decades ago—the statuesque, highly intelligent, and soft-spoken student who, in spite of her evident modesty, stood tall among her peers. Even then, she seemed destined for a future way beyond the norm. To see it being fulfilled is an absolute joy. I'm grateful to her for sharing this experience. I am thankful that, for a very brief moment, I was a passenger at some point along that journey, and I'm genuinely flattered to be afforded the privilege of writing this foreword so many years later. Thanks for the music, Rachael!

It would have taken a professional eye to detect any trace of the internal struggles swirling around in her young life. Outwardly, she remained happy, well-adjusted, and suitably mannered, though always slightly reserved. Above all, she radiated that ever-present drive—that internal motivation—to succeed, to conquer, and to excel.

Born in the US, Rachael came to Trinidad at a young age, to be schooled in her parents' native land. Her goals were evidently well set, and she pursued them vigorously, even as she soaked up the exotic, tropical lifestyle. After high school graduation, she returned to the US to serve in the army. I knew that should she never reestablish contact, I would somehow hear or even read about her again. It just didn't feel like an ending. She simply wasn't the type to cease and settle for a dull, monotonous routine. I knew, in the way that teachers instinctively do, that she was one destined for the billboards.

I confess to a tinge of sadness, but vindication, when she shared her personal journey of struggle, sometimes depression and despair, but ultimate accomplishment and triumph. Readers and soon-to-be followers are bound to find her book to be enthralling, emotional, and, above all, awesomely inspiring. Her mother and other close family members, I know, have all been integral instruments in her life's orchestra.

I feel sure there are even more intriguing chapters waiting to be written. Who knows where this absorbing story goes? Perhaps 1600 Pennsylvania Avenue? Don't you dare wager against this one!

As an award-winning playwright (Secondary School's Drama Festival, Prime Minister's Best Village Trophy Competition), writer (*Broadway Nights Mas on the Avenue*, 2019), PhD (ABD), and educator (30+ years), I am proud to welcome Rachael as a colleague in the literary world.

—James Baisden

Preface

I have withstood physical and emotional abuse, homelessness, and depression, so I write from a place of experience. I have been writing poetry since I was a teen; however, I decided to write this piece during the 2020 pandemic as mental health and domestic violence skyrocketed. It created a perfect opportunity for this type of story to be told. The stillness of life during this time allowed me to focus on defining my purpose to not be silent and bring awareness to such debilitating issues.

Introduction

Don't let anyone dim your spark! As a divorced single mother who feels paralyzed and is drowning with guilt and shame, it is never easy to start all over again. Family, friends, and coworkers may never understand the decisions she makes, but in reality they also don't know that she's trying to escape the pain. This is a fictional story about the life of a single mom who endures several challenges in her life and never gives up. Her journey is a roller coaster of emotions. Despite losing motivation from time to time, she musters the strength to endure the process. She overcomes traumatic experiences, struggles, and failures while celebrating her wins.

If you've ever felt betrayed, deceived, unloved, and rejected, then you can identify with the story. The plot contains consistent transference of despair between author and reader. RaeShelle is ill prepared for life's challenges as she fails miserably in a world that watches her with scrutiny. She has nine lives, and you will build a respect for her persistence. Imagine trying to ride a bike up a steep hill in inclement weather; making it to the top is a matter of life or death. Reserve the booster seat, secure your helmet, and prepare for this strenuous ride.

Never sit in silence when life is unbearable. Reach out for the necessary help you need to overcome and to heal. This book is not a cry for pity, but a journey through the trials of a single mother who refused to be a victim to her circumstances.

Chapter 1

It Failed and So Did She

Failure is a part of life, but it did not define RaeShelle's. After her US military career ended, she moved to Tobago for a while to spend some time with her friends and family. She needed to breathe and unwind from being deployed overseas. She enjoyed this time of freedom and frolicking, and it gave her awareness about what was next for her. Mom and Grandma were her grounding forces, and they knew she was now an adult and would make her own choices regardless. They both took the "I am going to pray for you" route, instead of dictating what her plan of action should be. The day she decided to leave home for the second time, she knew life was about to change.

She decided to move to New York on her twenty-first birthday without a plan. When she arrived in New York, Prospect Park was alive with drummers and vendors, and the water hydrants were ready for the city block excitement. The seasons were changing quicker than she could imagine. She survived somehow and lived with friends and relatives temporarily. She began to work a part-time job and realized she needed her own space. She got an affordable, low-income apartment in Brooklyn, which she called home. It was not much of a sanctuary because of the incessant noise of the streets, and the roaches crawling was unnerving, yet she felt a sense of pride. Nostrand Avenue was a street that never slept. She was now exposed to the criminal element, which manifested daily as dealers, users, sellers, and thieves. They lurked the streets as predators to take advantage of anyone who seemed vulnerable.

She was awakened the first day after moving into her new apartment by the wailing of the old man who helped her take her lamp up the stairs. The walls were so paper thin that she could hear the whole ordeal. The old man was being punched and kicked by the drug dealer across the hall for monies not paid the week prior. She was petrified. She was numb. She lay awake with the lights on for a week. Two weeks after moving in, she came home to a broken lock and a ransacked apartment. One of the thieves had broken in and stolen some cubic zirconia she had left on her nightstand. She kept her heirlooms on her person, always.

After a year of being single, she met Carlito in Queens while at a birthday party. He was a friend of a friend. They exchanged beeper numbers (yes, beepers in 1993), and they danced all night. The next day, they decided to meet for dinner. As they continued to date, within a couple of months, they were talking about moving into an apartment as a couple, and so they did.

By then she was pregnant, and they both seemed happy until Carlito began to change into someone she did not recognize. Despite her reservations, she agreed to marry him when their son, Junior, was two years old. She gave birth to their daughter, Faith, two years later, and she endured wedding blisters for about six years. She gradually realized that physical abuse was not a substitute for the American dream. She did not want her children to be raised in this dysfunction. RaeShelle decided that her safety was worth more than holding on to a false sense of hope. She never wanted her son to think that it was okay to abuse a woman and did not want her daughter to repeat the cycle. She had to make some hard decisions.

RaeShelle was aware of what she did not want; however, she overlooked the abuse for the sake of a fulfilled marriage. She was a loyal, resilient wife who was loved by her friends and family. She loved being loved at the beginning of their union, but of course, the red flags were evident. She ignored the signs. She dismissed Mr. Intuition. How could she be so vulnerable?

Although she was broken inside, RaeShelle presented strong confidence that was comforting to her soul. She felt the guilt of failing and the shame of ridicule. She felt the piercing stares and the judgmental whispers in her head.

She was now in an estranged marriage in New York City. She remembered many situations where she felt betrayed by the man who vowed to love, honor, and respect her. The deception was real. One day after Labor Day, she opened the window to a brisk, cool gale of fall wind. She decided she would dress both kids, pack a basket, and head to Central Park. At ages four and two, it took her about two hours to get them all ready for their field trip. From her five-story apartment, she could not see her red Nissan Sentra, which she had purchased on her own the year prior. She just knew it was where she parked it on Friday night. As the building she lived in had no elevator access, she gave her son, Junior, the task of holding the picnic basket. He struggled a bit, but he had to be her assistant. In tow, RaeShelle had the stroller, the baby bag, an Igloo cooler, and one-year-old Faith. When RaeShelle got to where she parked, she was a bit confused for a second. Her car was not where she left it. The world stopped revolving. Junior looked up at her as if to say, "Mom, what are we going to do?" She was numb. She did not know what to do. She called her estranged husband to ask for help with taking care of the children while she figured out her dilemma. He did not answer. He never answered. What was she thinking? He had neglected his duties as a father and a husband, and she stood alone with her children to face life's difficult situations. With her son looking directly at her, she quickly wiped her tears and called her friend Dee and her husband, Jay, to rescue her from a mental breakdown.

She did not call the authorities. Her gut feeling was right. She knew her husband was in the house the previous day. Things were moved, and more of his clothes were gone. She normally left her spare key for the Sentra in her jewelry chest, but it was missing. The key was missing. It was useless calling him. She got a weird phone call from a man claiming to be a DMV customer service representative. Apparently, a man in the DMV office had just bought the car from someone for $7,000 and was trying to switch titles. Illegal at its best. Her husband had orchestrated the plan. He was the mastermind behind the heist. He had someone steal her car and agreed to split the money with the thief. He sold it to an unsuspecting victim. RaeShelle felt betrayed and deceived, and yet she did not notify the authorities. She felt stupid. She did not want her children to learn later on in life that she had their father arrested for stealing her car. She had no idea what happened between Carlito and the buyer, but the next day her car and keys were returned. Her car was parked on the street in front of the apartment building, and the keys were left at the door. She did not ask any questions.

After that saga, she and her husband were not in a good place. She hated him for putting their family through this. There was no financial support, so she took advantage of the free benefits from the state in the form of cereal, cheese, milk, and eggs. That was a gift from the Divine. Her son's school fees were due monthly, and her daughter's daycare fees were due weekly. Rent was also due monthly. Her husband was responsible for half of the fees, as per their agreement, but that never happened. He refused to answer her calls because he knew she was calling to remind him of his obligation. He left the marital home, abandoned his family, and was now living with his new girlfriend.

When the going got tough, RaeShelle decided to think about her options. She was about six months behind on her rent, and one day there was a bright yellow sticker on the door, in plain sight for the other two neighbors to see. She was so ashamed. The eviction was here. It was time to decide.

As she reflected, she realized that she was an abused woman. The first slap to her face left her in utter disbelief. She felt the stinging force making contact with her left cheek. She looked into the mirror with tears in her eyes; she felt so ashamed. Her face was red and swollen with the imprint of five fingers, evidence that she had been slapped with force. She was so disappointed in herself that she cried in silence. Although they were estranged, there was physical and emotional abuse each time they interacted. She had been raped by this man whom she loved. She believed for so long that it was her fault. She was fearful that her children would also be abused, and she needed to protect them at all cost. With reservations, she agreed sometime afterward to allow the kids to visit him where he lived. She felt guilty that she had refused to let him see them, and if she did, it was only on her terms. She had a friend living nearby who kept a close eye on the activity at his place. By this time, she had shared with her cousin, who was a New York City cop, that she was having marital issues. She did not share the details because she was afraid of judgment.

This visitation ritual soon came to an abrupt end. RaeShelle was informed that her husband had moved unexpectedly, and he changed his phone number. He was selling drugs from his apartment and on some occasions while the kids were visiting. She was infuriated. She was afraid for her life and the lives of her children. Before he moved, she had to solicit the help of her cousin, the cop, to accompany her to get her children because her husband threatened never to return them to her. She felt threatened by the unknown and what ifs. What if she and the children were targeted because of his illegal activity?

That was it. This was the final determinant. She was convinced now more than ever that this was not where she wanted to be. She knew that her strength came from her ancestors. She knew that she had a strong family with robust values. She knew that her children were looking to her as supermom, to fix whatever was broken. She was committed to upholding the fact that failure was not a part of her family's legacy. She was responsible for her children's norms and belief system and did not want to pass on the feeling of failure to the next generation. She was the frontline. She was their first level of defense. She tried to protect them from the harsh reality of the truth, especially when they both saw her crying after a physical confrontation with him.

Understanding what was happening, her son asked, "Mom, are you okay?"

She responded with earnest hurt and emotional pain. "Yes, baby, Mom is okay. Mom and Daddy are okay, and our family will be okay."

Chapter 2

Hiding the Truth

Sometimes you live your life to protect other people's perceptions, and you lose your reality in the façade of a new normal. RaeShelle built a façade to hide her physical and emotional scars over the years. She was definitely serious about hiding the demons that were lurking in her home when Carlito still lived there. If the walls had eyes and ears, what would they whisper to her mother, sister, and friends when they came to visit? She was hoping that her mom, Elena, never became friends with her next-door neighbors because they would surely tell her the horrid truth.

Her children gave her strength. No matter how she tried to protect them, they had observed his meltdowns and the dysfunction regularly. She prayed that they were too young to remember. She knew it affected them at the time because her son was restless and emotional. Her daughter cried when she cried, even though she did not understand at one year old that Mom was an emotional wreck on the inside. One day, the roles were reversed. Her baby girl began wiping the tears rolling off her mother's face, while patting her on the back. RaeShelle felt the transference of her pain to her innocent baby girl, and she knew that this was unhealthy.

She realized the impact of the trauma caused by hiding the verbal, physical, and emotional abuse. It caused permanent scars, and she suffered from depression and anxiety. She was dishonest with her best friends and hid the feelings of despair, hurt, and fear from those close to her. RaeShelle remembered that one night, on a planned girls' night out in the summer, her best friend GiGi, observed that she had some bruising on her back as she zipped her up. GiGi stopped and used her fingers to touch the black and blue discolorations on RaeShelle's back. Before GiGi could even ask, RaeShelle shared a mere superficial excuse as a diversion.

She was looking forward to this party. They had already agreed to wear sleeveless and backless dresses. RaeShelle decided to wear a less flattering dress because she no longer felt stunning, and her self-esteem was nonexistent. She had to put on the Oscar-award-winning performance. She was in overdrive. Her friends were all disappointed that she wore a sleeved black dress instead of a brightly colored, revealing maxi she had bought specifically for that event. Her explanation did not align with the personality of a person they had grown to know and love, but as the night progressed, she overcompensated with high energy, laughter, and dancing. What began as a red-flag night dissolved into nothingness, and they all had a good time. No one knew.

On the way home from pretending she was on top of the world, the façade ended abruptly. As the valet stopped in front of the party of five, she said her goodbyes, tipped the valet, put on her seat belt, and waved gingerly to her friends with the window all the way up. The A/C and radio were already on. Her wedding song came on. She looked in the rearview mirror, and her friends were all out of sight. She could not hold it any longer. She could not drive. Her throat began to feel hot and swollen, and the tears were just uncontrollably flowing onto her dress. She pulled into a gas station not far from where she had just partied like a rock star. She was bawling and wailing at this point. RaeShelle was an emotional wreck. She could not stop crying and feeling hopeless. She thought about how much of a disappointment she was to her children because she was not fighting hard enough to get out of this dangerous situation, not just for herself but also for them. It took her two hours to pull herself together. By then, she realized she had six missed calls. All the girls were safely home and could not understand why she had not checked in like everyone else. She simply sent out a group text and lied. "I got home, showered, and fell asleep … sorry!"

She drove off and cried all the way home. Her will to fight never died. Years earlier, she had professional training in defensive tactics, and she decided to use the tools and discipline she learned to reframe her coping abilities. The shock of accepting that she was an abused woman was over, and she decided to do something about it. She had so many horrid memories. She remembered him punching her in the mouth in the presence of his mother and his aunt one day. His mother turned to her and asked, "What did you do?" RaeShelle could not believe his mother stood there watching it all unfold and still had the nerve to ask her that in disdain. His aunt then tried to give her a lesson in being a good wife.

She said, "Sometimes these things happen, and we have to just deal with them and move on." RaeShelle hated herself for allowing things to get this far.

When she got home, she wrote down every incident where she felt she was violated. She remembered being left in their apartment while she was pregnant, hungry with no food and no money to get food. She had beeped him several times. She waited all day until about six o'clock in the evening when she expected him to come home. That night, Carlito came home late, had already eaten, and swore that his beeper needed a battery. This was when hiding the truth could have been detrimental, not only to her but to her unborn child. Even after their first child was born, she remembered being slapped in front of his cousin, while holding her newborn. She was even pushed down the stairs while pregnant and went into premature labor. When asked about it, she lied. She did not tell anyone, including the doctor, why she was having pain. No one knew.

She began having visions of her late grandmother, Granny Aggie. They had shared a birthday, and their bond was strong. She remembered her grandmother praying at 5:00 every morning. Granny owned a book of prayers that was worn from daily use. She was unwavering and steadfast in her devotion. Granny always knew when something was wrong. After Granny Aggie died, RaeShelle still felt her presence, and she was ever so present during this time.

Similarly, her mom, Elena, always knew when to call. She always seemed to call after one of RaeShelle's emotional breakdowns. She always delivered a spiritually charged message, especially when she knew something was wrong. She never asked for details; she was just present and available. Her mom shared some biblical scriptures, affirmations, and hymns that her grandmother used to sing. This gave RaeShelle a renewed spirit.

Her faith was restored for the moment. She needed that. This interaction with her mom was confirmation that she had to act. She realized that she had to face her reality and choose to fight back instead of succumbing to the abuse of a coward. There was always a reason to fight back and never give up. Her reason was her children. She knew that holding on to an abusive relationship was not worth her life. When all else fails, God never fails. In this awakening and renewed faith, she knew that this was the beginning of a new chapter. Her childhood friend who lived in Atlanta encouraged RaeShelle and the kids to relocate and to escape.

Chapter 3

New Beginnings

Despite uncertainty, changing location may change your current situation. It certainly changed RaeShelle's. The Atlanta crew brought a dynamic to her life that she would never forget. Krissy rescued them from the New York saga. She took them in with no reservation.

RaeShelle developed a new personality to try to adapt to this new life as a single mother in a new city and to feel accepted in a place that never felt like home. She had to conform to single life as a single mother. This was new to her and to her kids. She was the only one of her friends in Atlanta with small children at the time, so she had to be a responsible mom, but she also wanted to frolic like everyone else. She had the full responsibility of child-rearing financially, physically, and emotionally. Even after she left New York City, the emotional abuse continued. In fact, her husband told her that she should use her "pussy" as a means to provide for *her* children and that no one would want to be in a relationship with her because she already had two children. Through it all, she hated her then husband for saying that. However, she had forgiven him, and more importantly, she had forgiven herself for ever giving him the power.

After moving and settling into single motherhood, she met a responsible teenage neighbor who she had developed a relationship with. She came occasionally to babysit the children for her. "Aunty Penny," as the kids called her, also took care of the children when RaeShelle wanted to go out with her friends. Even though she was outwardly enjoying the single life, a part of her being was inwardly dying, knowing she would rather be married to a man who wanted to help raise his children.

As a single woman, dating in a predominantly single community was easier than she thought. She did not always make the right choices, but she felt guilty that even though she was estranged from her husband before she left New York City, she was still legally married. It took her a while to actually say yes to a dinner date with someone for the first time. Prior to that, on several occasions, she agreed to go out on a date and then canceled the day of. This was all new to her, and it felt uncomfortable at first. Then she accepted that she needed to enjoy adult conversation and libations sometimes.

RaeShelle finally found a job and began socializing in a work environment. She had experienced prejudice from people of other races, and she managed the ignorance to some extent. However, she was saddened by her first encounter with her bank manager, who asked, "What's that on your head, curls?"

RaeShelle wanted to reply, "No, bitch, they're dreadlocks! Know anything about Bob Marley?" Instead, in her New York accent, she responded, "They are dreadlocks." The bank manager condescendingly grunted under her breath to the assistant manager, who looked at her in confusion. What made RaeShelle upset was that the manager was African American, but she had a negative perception of Caribbean American people with dreadlocks. *What? How ignorant!* What a difference between Northern versus Southern mentality.

This manager purposefully took RaeShelle out of the drive-thru teller position and placed her in the head teller/commercial teller position. RaeShelle told her she had a lot going on in her personal life and that she was not a good candidate at the time for that much responsibility. However, she needed her job, so she reluctantly agreed. She hated that position because it was an immense responsibility, and she did not know the other tellers very well. Because taking that position meant trusting others to be honest about running tickets, while giving and receiving cash in large amounts, she was cautious.

One day a dishonest teller who had been stealing from the bank didn't own up to taking $2,000 from RaeShelle and not writing or processing a ticket. The manager was aware of this teller's track record but did not take swift action. That same night, the teller took some blank cashier's checks and the $2,000 she stole and never came back to work. RaeShelle took the hit and was fired.

She felt alone sometimes, lonely. She missed her immediate circle of friends and her support system of friends from New York who also had children. Living in Atlanta was an adjustment she was not sure she could make overnight. She was consistent in finding weekend activities for the kids, and she set up play dates with other single moms in the area. Her daughter also had problems adjusting. RaeShelle went to pick up her daughter from day care on the day she had been fired from the bank, and the provider threatened to expel her daughter, if she did not stop biting the other children. Even though RaeShelle was coping with the loss of her job that day, she had to chuckle to herself. She had also been a biter in kindergarten.

Her relocation did not go as well as she planned, and she did not have a plan B. She needed a home of her own because she wanted her own space for her and her children. She did not want anyone to know she had lost her full-time job, and she did not want to ask for help. She definitely had to find another source of income to provide for her family, so she accepted part-time employment to make ends meet.

Chapter 4

The Hustle Is Real

It was definitely a balancing circus act. RaeShelle was a tightrope expert. She was walking a thin line, perfecting the skill of managing two jobs and two toddlers. She felt like her life was going nowhere, and she was a spinning top in mud. So confused by what life was delivering her, she felt the weight and the pressure of a thousand-pound demon on her shoulders. There was definitely a lesson to be learned, but she ignored the message. She needed to pivot. Her thoughts of lack, her beliefs, and her intentions did not align with the vision she had for herself.

RaeShelle was aware that her actions and her decisions affected the whole family. Losing her job triggered a fear of also losing control of her children and destroying their well-being. The kids were adopting bad habits from neighborhood children, on the bus, from their babysitter, and from their after-care companions. It was her fault. Everyone else around her was raising her children because she was always at work. She had to get a grip. Her life was spiraling out of control. She was teaching at a local school during the day and cleaning offices at night. Both children were acclimating to new friends and new relationships, but RaeShelle felt that because of her decisions, she had destroyed their childhood and it was her fault that they had a broken relationship with their dad. She wanted to start making more sound, logical decisions so that her life could have some semblance of structure.

Even with two jobs, she struggled. She visited the local pantries and churches for food on Saturdays with the children. They were happy to take a weekly field trip and to choose the goodies, fruits, and veggies they liked. She tried to make it as fun as possible, while dying inside. This distribution came from local supermarkets and grocers and was donated to the churches and the less fortunate. She had to accept the help, although she was ashamed. While waiting in line, she hid from people she recognized.

Both of her roommates were buying homes, which meant that she was on her own. She was in a panic. In desperation, she decided to apply for a home loan. She knew she had to be positive about her goal of homeownership, but the reality was that she had two jobs that barely paid the bills. Her friend Allysa looked over her finances, and she convinced her to apply even if she felt unsure. At least she would be advised on how to be proactive in order to be approved if she was denied this time around. The reality was she needed a better-paying job. She was denied the opportunity for homeownership, and she was devastated, knowing she was working on a timeline. Her faith was being tested. Elena always seemed to know when she needed spiritual guidance. The day RaeShelle got the disappointing news, her mom called to pray with her, not knowing what her daughter had just experienced.

RaeShelle had both a fear of failure and the faith that she had what it took to make homeownership a possibility. She had the willpower to give this vision all of her focus. Faith and fear could not coexist in her world anymore. She had to believe it to achieve it. She started believing it was never too late to change course, and she had to do things differently to get a different result. She had to submit to the idea that she needed the help and strength of the two people she trusted: her mom and her sister Gen. She really needed their support to remain in that positive space. Until then, she was in survival mode only.

Chapter 5

Progress

When one door slams and hits you in the face, be ready to kick it wide open. It was no coincidence that RaeShelle's mother and sister ended up living with her just when she needed them. She did not have a home, and they were aware that her roommates were only there temporarily until they moved out. Elena and Gen were on a mission to be her strength. It could not have been a more perfect alignment of her vulnerability and them coming to her rescue. They always seemed to read between the lines of her struggles. Family was everything, and she knew the universe, her Divine, her Higher Power, was looking out for her. Her sister knew she needed a free babysitter in order to reach her home-buying goals, and she stepped in immediately.

RaeShelle trusted her sister and her mom with the nurturing of her children. She never questioned their intentions or ability to raise her children, especially when she was too busy working. She was already afraid of losing her children to the influence of others and felt relieved that her mother's strength was grounding, and her sister's unconditional love encouraged her to keep moving forward. The pivot she needed involved trusting the process. It involved focus. It involved having faith. She had to surrender to the idea of accepting help, financially, emotionally, and spiritually.

Her mom and sister moved permanently to Atlanta. It had been six months since RaeShelle was denied a mortgage loan. She reached out to a real estate agent who had an awesome team, and she was open to being coached and guided by the experts. She was grateful and felt that as soon as she changed her mindset, things in her life would begin to change.

Not long after, she was accepted in a lottery for a first homebuyer program. She could not believe it. Her friend Ethel invited her to dinner one day to show RaeShelle what her neighborhood looked like. RaeShelle envisioned herself living there with her children. She was not sure how this miracle was going to unfold, but she had faith. A week after she and RaeShelle had dinner at Norson Lake Community, Ethel called her breathless with excitement. There was a paper announcement in the community center, advertising the sale of a home that was available not far from where Ethel lived. RaeShelle immediately called her agent, excited.

She was going to be a homeowner at twenty-nine as a single mother. She was proud of herself. She worked through her self-doubt and worry, and she delivered security on a platter to her children. This was her first home, and this was a major accomplishment. They now had a home of their own and individual rooms where they could build memories for themselves.

It was definitely a blessing to have her family around her, and even though she worked two jobs, it was evident that her children were being nurtured and loved unconditionally by Grandma Elena and Aunty Jen. Her mom took pride in decorating the house and the windows every chance she got. That Halloween she and Gen were happy to dress the children in costumes and take them out into the streets to get candy from the neighbors. The kids were so happy.

Grandma Elena was so grateful to spend quality time with them, and Gen enjoyed seeing the kids happy.

Although the family had their challenges, they made it work. There was just one car in the house. Gen dropped their mom off to work first at 5:00 a.m., Junior next to the bus stop at 7:00 a.m., and then RaeShelle, Gen, and Faith headed about twenty miles south to the preschool where they worked and Faith attended. At night, they did the reverse. It was a demanding schedule, but they made it work. RaeShelle worshiped every morning to the music of BeBe and CeCe Winans. The kids sometimes watched her wipe the tears away when she felt overwhelmed, but she was grateful things were improving. This was her miracle, and she was hopeful that this momentum would last. Even in adversity, she knew it was not too late to spark the fire within. It was nothing short of a miracle that her mom and sister's intervention was Divine and on time. They created the shield she needed to build the resilience to face her pending divorce.

Chapter 6

Divorced and Broken

Never underestimate the power of the D. It was the devil. RaeShelle filed for divorce, and it was absolutely warranted, but she felt it with every fiber of her soul. She knew it was time, and her mind was set. She contacted an old friend and attorney from New York City. He represented her well, and before she knew it, she was divorced. She felt the guilt and shame all over again when she received the certified copies in the mail.

However, this was a constant reminder of living with regret. She knew nothing happened before its time, and nothing happened by chance. It was painful, not because she was sad she and her husband were not together as a couple, but she was hurt and angry that the family structure she worked so hard to mold was not as important to him as it was to her. She needed this for her children. She also knew that even though the marriage was officially over by law, she had to work on her past trauma during the marriage and the painful regrets that were a reminder every time she struggled emotionally or financially. She was not yet ready.

She was finally dealing with the emotional loss of the head of household, even though he never played the role of the head, even before their daughter was born. They had been estranged since then. This meant a loss of communication, a loss of potential financial support, and a loss of a father's love. She knew what that felt like. She grew up visiting with her dad once a month at Grandma Aggie's front gate with minimal conversation. She questioned whether she made the right decision of escaping the claws of abuse for the sake of family. She did not know how to console her spirit. She did not know how to soothe her soul. Her thoughts were racing. She wanted to talk to the children about it, but would they understand as toddlers? Did they remember the fights and punches? Did she want them to relive the trauma?

Everything was her responsibility. She had no financial help from the ex, and it was a challenge. She was afraid of failing at life, and most of all, she was afraid of failing at being a mother. If she could not pay her bills and lost her house and car, her ex-husband would ridicule her for being a bad mother. The children would hate her for having to move again after making friends and building relationships. She had the biggest responsibility of being the head of household, and she was petrified. She had just bought a home. She was supposed to be on a natural high. Elena and Gen were giving her love and support, but she was broken. She was in a black hole. She had to find a way to survive. Her financial instability was a secret. Her friends and family had no idea that she was struggling emotionally and financially. Each month, she had to shuffle money around to make things work. Both of her jobs were part time, and she knew she was heading into hardship. Her self-doubt and insecurity about what was next were taking their toll on her mental health.

One day, she drove into the driveway, and the sensor light never came on. The power and light company was tired of waiting for their money. When her electricity was turned off, the embarrassment destroyed any sliver of dignity she had left. RaeShelle saw the look in her mother's eyes. She wished the earth could open and swallow her up. She said nothing. Her mom said, "We will go to the office tomorrow to make the payment. I am here for you." RaeShelle went to her room, too ashamed to speak.

She was depressed. She cried herself to sleep behind closed doors. This fear was real. The shame was real. She imagined what her mom and sister may have been thinking about her now that she was divorced. They were there when she got married. They were a part of her wedding, and now it was all over. This divorce deflated her strength and made her withdrawn and helpless.

Chapter 7

Exhausted by Life

Fatigue possessed her mind, her body, and her soul. Shutting down and running away from unresolved problems leads to dead-end solutions. RaeShelle felt as if boulders were being thrown at her, hitting the most vulnerable parts of her body with no shield. She felt the pain of the old bruises and recurring pains of the fresh, open wounds. She felt the urge to run and never look back.

Her two-job marathon came to a screeching halt. She had been working overtime daily and only getting three to four hours of sleep per night. She went to one job early one morning, did a double shift, and then reported to her second job at 4:00 p.m. After working six hours, she was relieved at 10:00 p.m. She left work with the intention of getting some milk at the local grocer's and then heading home to rest. She stopped at the traffic light, and that was all she remembered. She fell asleep behind the wheel and had an accident. Working two jobs took a terrible toll on her health. This accident almost took her life.

RaeShelle woke up in a strange place with bright lights. She tried to talk and couldn't. As she opened her eyes slowly, she recognized her mom at her bedside, huddled over with both hands clasped together as if she were praying. RaeShelle did not know what was happening or why she was lying there unable to move any part of her body. She wanted her mom to see that she was awake, but she could not verbalize. She tried to move parts of her body, but nothing happened. At this point, she was just grateful that she was able to open her eyes. She groaned, and her mom immediately woke up. She cried tears of joy. She had been praying incessantly. RaeShelle was conscious, and all the floor nurses ran in. It would take a medical team and eight months of therapy to put her back together again.

What's hidden in the dark always finds a way of surfacing. She had been hiding the fact that she had recently applied for government assistance. The accident set her back eight months. She was behind in her mortgage payments and her car payments, and she kept this a secret from everyone. Elena and Gen were taking care of the children and the household bills, and for this, she was eternally grateful. What a blessing they were to her while RaeShelle was in recovery and underwent a series of small operations to repair damage caused by the accident.

It was a shock when one day RaeShelle was served a notice of foreclosure via the mail carrier, which her sister signed for. This was definitely a call for a family meeting, where she had to divulge all of her financial woes. This was her chance to purge and to realize that the only way out of this situation was to be totally transparent with the people who were supporting her unconditionally. She had to stop running away and disconnecting from things that made her uncomfortable.

She was forced to do some soul searching and introspection. Looking in the mirror was difficult. It meant facing the unavoidable truth. Surviving this near-death experience was a premonition of a purpose. She knew she had lived through this tragedy for a reason. What was that reason? She had to find purpose in her pain. She knew she had to use her story one day to help others. This was not all in vain.

She knew making the same decisions over and over would yield the same results that, up to this point, proved to be futile. Giving up was not an option. Running away from her situation would lead to dead-end solutions. This reality was a fierce one to swallow. She changed her norm.

RaeShelle discussed some new plans she had been thinking about with her mother and sister. She shared with them that she did not feel grounded in Atlanta and needed a change of pace. Although she was battered by her circumstance, RaeShelle's reality forced her to activate her inner warrior to conquer the fight of her life. She was fortunate enough to have the support of her sister, who was up for relocating and embracing the change.

Her mom was skeptical and worried, but she put all of her concerns in God's hands.

Chapter 8

Fight or Flight

At the cliff! Time to jump! There is no turning back! Mom decided to return to Tobago to take care of her jewelry business, and RaeShelle and Gen decided to relocate to Texas. RaeShelle did not let landing in the ghetto determine the outcome of her experience. She was adjusting to the roller coaster of life.

She became really dependent on her sister's logic and support. She had little confidence in her own ability. Her insecurities were embedded in her mindset that she still wasn't enough. She remembered that even after packing the U-Haul truck with hours left to leave Atlanta, she had no idea where they were going to live. She had done some preliminary research on apartment homes, but she did not have the down payment required. While driving to Texas, she contacted Dee, an old friend, who lived there years prior. She shared with him that she had lost her house to foreclosure in Atlanta, and that she had to get away from the memory of failure. Dee knew someone with accommodations, but nothing was available at the time. The landlord promised that the room would be available in a week. During this time they were homeless, but Dee did what he promised. He paid two months' rent for them to live until they were able to figure things out. The apartment was worn and dirty. The carpet was soiled, the damaged green bathtub was plugged with newspaper and plastic bags to avoid critters from crawling in at night, and the wall unit air conditioner housed rats and roaches.

Ironically, RaeShelle was now faced with the same drug activity she feared in New York. It was the same drug activity that her ex exposed their children to, and it was infecting her space once again. This was not at all what she wanted for her children. Her ex-husband knew that she was attempting to receive child support, and he moved from state to state, trying to evade the process. If her ex-husband had acted like the man she expected him to be, she would not be in this situation. She hated him for that. Although she lived in less than perfect conditions, her kids were happy in the courtyard where they lived. They found new friends to play with and created new bonds that they did not experience in Atlanta. They played all day long until they were tired. RaeShelle feared that if she found a job, her kids would be left home alone, and this scared her.

The bankruptcy and the foreclosure of the Atlanta property made it really difficult for RaeShelle to find a job; therefore, her sister became the main breadwinner in the family. As time progressed, unfortunately for RaeShelle, Gen found love in Texas and ultimately planned to move out within the year. It was an inevitable race for RaeShelle to get on her feet before the hourglass trickled the passage of time. She made appointments with several temp agencies and scheduled several interviews every day to increase her chances of job placement. Now the tables were turned. She remembered as children growing up, she was Gen's protector and her guide, but now Gen was her support and her voice of reason. She was torn between feeling happiness for Gen and feeling lost without her.

This was a challenge, especially now that Gen was moving to a new city. RaeShelle knew that she had to face it head-on and realized that she had to use the momentum she had built for herself to keep moving forward and not look back. Resilience became her way of life. Once her sister moved out, RaeShelle knew she was going to be on her own. She was aware that her children were watching her strength. One day, her son told her that he admired how she made things happen for them, despite the circumstances. The only way out was up.

Chapter 9

Onward and Upward

Education was RaeShelle's only way out of the ghetto, and welfare was the segue to success. In this instance, RaeShelle swallowed her pride one day and walked to the Department of Children and Families, hoping not to see anyone she knew. She was humiliated and anxious. She was introduced to Mrs. Islas, who immediately recognized that RaeShelle was ashamed. Mrs. Islas made her comfortable by asking her about future goals and aspirations. RaeShelle was assigned a case manager who cared about her and her children and delivered two beds to the ghetto for RaeShelle and her children, which were donated by the local church.

RaeShelle prayed for the opportunity to return to school and to achieve success. She kept working on a positive mindset by creating a vision board with the dynamics of her life she envisioned and having the faith that it all would come to fruition. Two weeks after RaeShelle and her counselor met, she was given the opportunity to start at a community college. She figured out the secret formula of maximizing an educational opportunity, which would lead to her success. She was now a full-time student majoring in criminal justice administration. She was promised a $500 incentive for finding a job and keeping it for six months. Mrs. Islas was so gracious that she referred her to a state job. During her transition from welfare to working a state job, her case manager provided her with gas cards so she could get to and from work.

She was afforded a promotion. All the while, she remained humble, and she continued her education to get a bachelor's and a master's degree. Because of her education, she was able to compete and qualify for the job she wanted.

The female counselor, Mrs. Islas, played matchmaker and introduced RaeShelle to a colleague. Soon they started dating and RaeShelle fell in love with Mat. He was able to move them out of the ghetto. In order to show her children who were now ten and eight years old a great example, Mat and RaeShelle dated and then got married, before moving into their apartment together. Not long after their union, they were able to purchase their first home. The kids loved him dearly. He was the perfect dad and cared about their well-being, as much as he cared about their mother's. She decided to give this relationship her all.

This was the family structure RaeShelle had wanted and needed, not only for herself but for her children. They were definitely living the American dream as a family. They planned family trips together, and RaeShelle's mom and sister came along sometimes. Her son formed such a bond with his stepdad that it was remarkable to see them together playing golf and watching football games.

Because she knew the importance of education and how it benefited her after such a long period of misfortune, RaeShelle pursued her PhD. She intended to be an example to her children. She displayed strength. Even while raising a family, she endured and achieved a great accomplishment. She definitely used the resources that were available at the time to build a better life for her and her family. RaeShelle used education as a tool to climb out of the ghetto and to help her mom financially as much as she could. That was the least she could do.

Her gratitude gave her the strength to keep going even when life was not perfect. She had her own struggles within her marriage, but this time, she was more resilient.

Her educational goals forced her to have tunnel vision. Her husband did not understand her drive to succeed, and she ignored his feelings of neglect. They grew apart, and she felt increasingly alone.

RaeShelle began using the resources and skills she had developed during her struggles to be resilient. She was more confident now than before that even if her marriage did not work, she now had the coping skills and an education to move forward. Climbing the success ladder was invigorating, but her relationship decisions were less than perfect.

Chapter 10

Yet Another Hurdle

Turning a blind eye to God's design was RaeShelle's demise. Although her marriage now seemed to be on solid ground, she quickly realized that building a family without a strong foundation was a recipe for disaster.

She always remembered Granny Aggie as she talked about couples in the neighborhood being unequally yoked, but she never understood as a child growing up what she meant. When RaeShelle became a vacation Bible school teacher as a young adult, she learned from the junior pastors at church how important it was to marry someone with a similar belief system. This came to mind when her second marriage began unraveling, especially when they argued on a Sunday morning. He was not going to church, and there was nothing she could do about it. There were so many red flags before she actually took that leap of faith to remarry. The signs were there. They were so obvious, but she did not pay attention on purpose. He was an atheist, and she was Christian, so raising the kids in a household where parent and stepparent had different value systems was a challenge. She prayed and took the kids to church, and he refused to go with them at all. He did not celebrate any of the religious holidays, and she felt that she was walking on eggshells whenever the topic came up. Then there was the deception.

One day, her husband withdrew $700 from their joint bank account, which was meant only to pay bills. She never got an explanation of where the money went.

There was definitely something else going on besides the truth. The spiritual warfare and financial stressors put a consistent rift between them both. She later found out that there were three children he never told her about. That was definitely the end of her patience. She was ready and willing to repair the family finances to make things work until she found out that he had been lying the whole time. She was frustrated and angry that this had happened again. She had been on the same path five years ago in her last marriage. Once again, the person she loved had deceived her. She began blaming herself for loving too soon, not giving herself enough time to heal from her past.

At about the seven-year mark, she started to hate her situation. She was angry because of the financial difficulties, and they defaulted on the mortgage just when the housing market crashed. They couldn't refinance at a lower mortgage rate. It came to the point where even their housing association fees were in arrears.

One day she was unable to get into her gated community because they had cut all access. She had to enter as a guest and wait in line to be processed instead of simply driving in. That was so embarrassing. Her husband was responsible for making that payment. He had not paid in nine months. When she asked him about it, there was no answer.

These were definitely irreconcilable differences. They drifted apart, and eventually, the inevitable happened. She told him to leave, so he got an apartment and moved out. She was so embarrassed, hurt, and frustrated that she could not stay. She looked for an apartment that was more convenient for her and the kids to get to and from school. She felt dejected. This was a vicious cycle of another failed marriage. She decided to go to therapy to work on her acceptance of her new reality; at least she knew that she now had a career and an education as a backup. She started eating incessantly. After gaining thirty pounds and being diagnosed with high cholesterol, she decided to really watch her diet and exercise with a friend who owned a gym. She began relying on and trusting her ability to be resilient despite the odds.

RaeShelle had a confidence like never before. She had her career and her education, which gave her the boost she needed to move on.

Chapter 11

Full Throttle Ahead

RaeShelle was beating the odds methodically, one move at a time. It's not how you start but how you finish the race. She was now divorced but stronger than she was the first time. She realized that being a single mother to two teenagers took a different type of skill and Divine intervention. Elena could not help because she was busy with her jewelry business in Tobago, and Gen was in Texas, living a good life with her new husband.

Teenagers brought a different vibe to the equation. There was a lot of financial stress simply because each teen now wanted a car. She was now responsible for car insurance, life insurance, and medical insurance, and she became really frustrated because there was still no help from her ex. Above all, college was right around the corner for both of the children. She was also really concerned about leaving a legacy for them. Her third home was a miracle. She had already decided that she was not about to attempt homeownership again, especially as a single mother. She had enough on her plate. Her boss, Marie, gave her some sound advice, and she decided to purchase a home once the kids were both out of high school. She had a tour of this same house months before with both kids and her Realtor. It was still under contract by a couple who was having loan approval issues. She had faith. She prayed for this house silently. Ironically, RaeShelle and Marie were having cocktails for her birthday at Marie's retirement home on the beach when the Realtor called. The house was back on the market. RaeShelle left the beach that evening and did one more walk-through that night. Her Realtor placed an offer the next day. By March, she was a homeowner once again. Even after welfare, bankruptcy, and foreclosure, RaeShelle was able to buy a third house.

The kids were now adults and making their own decisions about life. She was grateful that she had been an example to them throughout their lives, and they had chosen to be educated, kind, independent, strong, and ambitious. She loved that they were both critical thinkers and were not easily swayed. Despite their individual challenges as adults, they knew that RaeShelle had set the foundation for their future. Because of her struggles and accomplishments, and because they had witnessed her progression, they blossomed into a better version of their mother. That's all a mother can ask for.

Shortly after becoming a new homeowner, RaeShelle decided to open her own business. She felt the need to keep adding to her portfolio of life. Although she had a career in the mental health field, she also wanted to be a boutique owner—a gateway to reaching other single parents and sharing her story of hope and empowerment. Now that the children had gone off to live their own lives in different states, she was an empty nester. She welcomed the new change even though she missed them. She was busier now than she was when they were teens at home. FaceTime, Zoom, and WhatsApp videos made the distance painless. For her, it was actually more fun watching them function as adults, but the best part was that she got to give them advice based on her own experiences. So rewarding!

RaeShelle decided to share her story in several magazines both locally and internationally. She was so proud to gift one of the magazines to her mom and sister. They had experienced the entire saga from beginning to end. They were even more elated that they got to be a part of her happiness. Her success story could empower others. All things are possible. There is nothing that can stand in the way of a woman who has learned from her mistakes.

Resilience and faith had empowered this single mother after she had experienced homelessness, depression, and hopelessness. She still had the strength to overcome. She never submitted to her failures.

If you are in a similar situation, do not be afraid or ashamed to reach out for help. Abuse is never okay. Resources are available online, through doctor's referrals, support groups, and churches.

Get help! "…with God all things are possible" (Matthew 19:26).

Biography

Rachael Ann Riley is a mental health professional with a PhD (ABD) in forensic psychology. She is the author of the e-book *Building Resilience After Divorce or Breakup*. She spent several years mentoring abused single women living in shelters, while on their journey to establishing a new healthy lifestyle. Rachael also spent more than seven years working as a mental health professional in the federal prison system, where she offered therapy and group sessions to the system's most vulnerable inmates. She uses her experience as a domestic violence survivor and single mother to empower women across the world.

Fear of failure stifles the meek at heart, but faith helps create the confidence needed to build resilience.

Single parents sacrifice their hearts and souls providing for their families as they work through depression, shame, and guilt. At times, many of them wrestle with low self-esteem, homelessness, and hopelessness, and question their will to continue living a nightmare. It is never easy to raise children alone and even harder to beg for support from the non-custodial parent.

I Am Enough is a riveting story about strength and determination that will empower single parents with tools to strengthen their faith, increase their ability to set goals, and practice persistence. In this memoir, Rachael walks readers through the adversities of a divorced mom who overcomes struggles and challenges. She personifies resilience and is an inspiration to those who have lost hope along the way.

The author is a mental health professional and domestic violence survivor. She also served as a mentor to abused single women living in shelters while on their journey to establishing a new healthy lifestyle.

Family is the most powerful unit in the world, but at times, it can be fractured if managed by one guardian. If you are financially, spiritually, and emotionally drained as a single parent, *I Am Enough* is the tool you need to refocus and regain your strength.